Bezdelki

Poems and Translations in Memory of
Yuri Georgievich Drobyshev, 1932-2015

OTHER BOOKS FROM THE EMMA PRESS

THE EMMA PRESS PICKS

The Flower and the Plough, by Rachel Piercey
The Emmores, by Richard O'Brien
The Held and the Lost, by Kristen Roberts
Captain Love and the Five Joaquins, by John Clegg
Malkin, by Camille Ralphs
DISSOLVE to: L.A., by James Trevelyan
The Dragon and The Bomb, by Andrew Wynn Owen
Meat Songs, by Jack Nicholls
Birmingham Jazz Incarnation, by Simon Turner

POETRY PAMPHLETS

Mackerel Salad, by Ben Rogers
Trouble, by Alison Winch
Dragonish, by Emma Simon
Pisanki, by Zosia Kuczyńska
Who Seemed Alive & Altogether Real, by Padraig Regan
Paisley, by Rakhshan Rizwan

POETRY ANTHOLOGIES

The Emma Press Anthology of the Sea
This Is Not Your Final Form: Poems about Birmingham
The Emma Press Anthology of Aunts

SHORT STORY COLLECTIONS

First fox, by Leanne Radojkovich
Postcard Stories, by Jan Carson
The Secret Box, by Daina Tabūna

BEZDELKI

Small things by Carol Rumens
Illustrations by Emma Wright

THE EMMA PRESS

For Yura

☙

THE EMMA PRESS

First published in Great Britain in 2018
by the Emma Press Ltd

Text © Carol Rumens 2018
Illustrations © Emma Wright 2018

All rights reserved.

The right of Carol Rumens and Emma Wright to be
identified as the author and illustrator respectively of this work
has been asserted by them in accordance with the Copyright,
Designs and Patents Act 1988.

ISBN 978-1-910139-80-6

A CIP catalogue record of this book
is available from the British Library.

Printed and bound in Great Britain
by Charlesworth Press, Wakefield.

The Emma Press
theemmapress.com
queries@theemmapress.com
Jewellery Quarter, Birmingham, UK

☙

*'Bread, beer, oxen, birds, my heart being
sweet… cause me to carry to you anything –'*
from Taharqa's Prayer to Amun-Ra.

'Душа ведь женщина, ей нравятся безделки…'
The soul's a woman, you know, the small things matter…
from 'When Psyche-life…', by Osip Mandelstam

☙

ЮРА (YURA)

You: someone I almost didn't ring.
You: whose sadness I fell into.
You, yes you: I broke your sadness, laughing
nervously: yes, me. Lights on, warm kitchen. You
always on Sunday nights. Then half a lifetime.
You, zaichik moi. You, smaller, funnier,
the farther off you go. You looking back as I
look back. You saying 'Come on, come on!'
You I can never outlive. My inmost you.
My I and I. Ah, deepest IOU.

Contents

'When Psyche-life follows Persephone...' 1
Bezdelki, with Morphine 2
Equipped 4
He Drank to Naval Anchors 6
The Admiralty 8
King Taharqa's Last Thoughts 9
Shapka and Spider 14
Collection Plate 15
At Four Monthes Mind, no Requiem 17
Summer Visitor 18
Vidua 19
Diaspora 21
Nant y Garth 23

Notes 25
Acknowledgements 26
About the poet 27
About the illustrator 27
About the Emma Press 28

'When Psyche-life follows Persephone…'

When, through translucent forest, Psyche-life
follows Persephone down into the dark,
a sightless swallow flings itself in her path
with angry tenderness, and a twig in leaf.

The shades rush round to greet the visitor.
They cry their miseries to a new-found friend
and wring their feeble hands in bewilderment
and timid longing, stretching out to her.

One offers her a mirror, one, a phial of scent.
The soul's a woman, you know, the small things matter.
Over the sterile woods, their voices patter
like dry rain-drops, equally transparent.

The soul's confused by all this tender fussing.
The glassy oaks, she thinks, must be a dream;
she breathes onto the mirror, takes her time
fumbling out her coin for the misty crossing.

Bezdelki, with Morphine

I don't know what you dreamt of – your first fuck
or the last teaspoon-sip of strawberry yoghurt?
Perhaps you waved your grey and faithful stick
or some enchanting "find", some tiny engine-part.

Your breath came fast and steadily; when less
than audible, I thought it only sleep's
new, uneventful phase. Later, I fetched the glass
and held it to your mouth. I kissed your lips

and felt, this time, no little answering pull,
the reflex of reflection, two-as-one.
(Don't worry: shades, you know, are kissable.)
I woke my phone. The compact's swing-glass shone.

I don't know in what currency you paid,
or if you saw the leafless crystal oaks,
or if a mist came down, or a mist cleared,
as the ferryman and you exchanged small jokes…

Thus Psyche-life, who studied animation
at a fine film-school, storyboards the sequel,
a short montage for the remotest reel
far beyond metaphor and adaptation.

She's your material girl: there's lots to do.
She finishes the yoghurt, washes spoons
and sheets, dusts mirrors, picks up small possessions
like clouds, and watches them turn into you.

Equipped

In the cupboard where I've been sent,
I could play Sudoku,
make stews and *pirogi,* drink beer,
look at old Christmas cards
and *discover the explosive origins of the galaxies, stars and planets.*

In this thoughtfully furnished afterlife,
I could re-thread a strimmer;
I could drill holes in concrete;
I could inhibit a year's worth of headaches
and still have pills enough for the perfect suicide.

I'm beginning to know how they felt,
the Egyptian royals, wakeful
in their scratchy bandages;
their small feasts rotting around them, papyri rustling
with nauseating spells for fresh supplies.

Hundreds of loyal shabti
are ready to embark at a minute's notice
on the new irrigation system you'll design
next spring, my Lord Beloved. After a month of glazed
un-helpful stares, his Lordship rather doubts it.

A girl strips to her muscles,
stumbles around to find the make-up slate.
It's heaped with her living colour –
but suddenly she doesn't see the point,
and wearily lies down again.

There's one warm face she still mirrors,
one fluid look, one undemanding smile.
She wonders about him. She tries
not to think he's out there somewhere,
being sad for her, or perhaps beyond being sad.

He Drank to Naval Anchors

And he drank to Marxism-Leninism and fridge-freezers.
And he drank to Capitalism and struggling repair-men.

He drank to beer-bottle-tops and hermaphrodite bread-bags,
half brown paper, half crisp cellophane,

to bison stock-cubes and Ardennes duck-pâté,
and the gold braid twisted into reproachful anchors

on salt-white caps no Soviet sailor wore.
He drank to James Bond and to Stephen Hawking.

To spattered Reeboks and to chain-store sweaters
with Pure Wool XL labels, he drank deep

the sweet fermented brew of the charity shops.
He folded all his maps. This was world culture.

Nowhere called him back and nowhere beckoned.
He drank to the gods: Schastliviye Puti!

And he drank to Marxist-Leninism and fridge-freezers.
And he drank to Capitalism and struggling repair-men.

The Admiralty

In the Northern capital, dusty *populus*,
Sighing, mantles the time's transparency
And, through green dark, a frigate or an acropolis,
Brother to water and sky, glows distantly.

A boat of air, its mast like a touch-me-not –
To Peter's progeny this rule declares
Beauty was never the whim of a demi-god,
But a simple carpenter's calculating stares.

Four good elements rule us, but mankind
Is free; we've raised a fifth to pride of place:
Doesn't an ark so faultlessly designed
Repudiate the sovereign claims of space?

Cranky medusas consolidate a position,
Anchors' abandoned ploughs are adrift in rust –
But look, the three dimensions burst from their prison
And all the world's seas are open to us at last.

King Taharqa's Last Thoughts

When the Pharaoh wants the war,
the war wants the Pharaoh.
When the Pharaoh wants the war no longer,
he sinks into the sand, already a sphinx,
and the drum, the drum he hates more than the war-drum
(who's banging it so hard, his weightless heart?)
slips away from his chest, devolves to footfall.

*

Dawn. Sole-beat and water-song.
The river my sister sings the shape of herself,
leaps where lion-I leaps, dances past the lion
on his short rope, appetite:
sometimes pretends to do nothing –
marsh-maker, rock-sucker, sky-mirror,
word-weaver, choked with papyrus;
rouses again, and races the lion-man's racing:
foam-fleck, foot-flash, rainbow-flake, two of us neck-and-neck,
slipping past settlements, slopping in rock-pools, black
and white in the crash-sites, slow and snakeskin-yellow
through Memphis into *hundred-gated Thebes*.

The Kushite cub, nosing in the ruins,
feels a hand on his shoulder   finds himself kneeling –
*bread, beer, oxen, birds, my heart being sweet   cause me
to carry to you anything* –

and the same hand opens, slides an arpeggio
of light on the toppled pillars,
and taps in my head seven syllables: *carry to me my city.*

*

The unfledged papyrus sighs
for water, twisting its toes
in rusty canopic silt
and the beached skiff prays for a river, for you, Amun,
Amun, who drops, who rises
      when the
            Pharaoh
                  wants the
                          war
and when the Pharaoh wants the war no longer,
and sags to his hip-bone, prayerless,
his sweet heart sucked by five Assyrian arrows.

*

Souls clatter like wings,
like netted marsh-birds, blind
to everything but their sky.

Was this your lion army
or mine, Esarhaddon?
The dead grin up at our flags.
They belong to no state, no species.

Croak with the broken ibis, Pharaoh. Howl with the
   soldiers' wives.

*

When I woke, it was only this world.
Thin waves came in from nowhere, rippling the dunes.
The dead rolled over, *ignes fatui*,
and the moonlit boat appeared, dragging threads of new river.
I felt a hand on my shoulder   felt that muscle
of air in the silk-cool desert-night. Amun
(wiser than Xerxes) wanted
it seemed   to call off the war   no longer wanted
a king who wanted a war   (or a war that wanted a god).

*

Taharqa, already a sphinx,
moves his eyelids, remembering.

*

At first, we were playing a game. We joked and jostled,
but we knew our race would become
a temple, we felt that darkness.
Soon, with a fiercer beat and concentration,
we ran, just ran   ran on   ran on and on   our lungs
high lyres   we scrubbed the burning from our eyes
which filled and burned again   the smears of palm-trees
were ghosts, we thought, not messengers. And then

the victor crashed the finishing rope, and flung
himself across, and we all
flung ourselves across, broken with laughter
and moaning, lightly-wounded pride the same
for slave and king, runner-up and also-ran.

We praised each other, thanked the gods, we plunged
our mouths in bowls of pomegranate wine.
Amun was writing on the broken stelae
of ripples where we skinny-dipped, and each
to his own hot floating face said the god's name.

*

By the river that rises in the Otherworld
where everyone's god is his heart, mixing him freshly
from blood and darkness
                       drumming him upwards
                                   drumming him
to wake to a new forgetting,
I become the scratch of script, the scribe's light re-construction:

He flung the molten ball Jerusalem
to you, the future. Memphis, he returned
to the gods. He won a kingdom
lovely as waterfalls; he lost a desert.
He liked to run, Taharqa: he ran with his men.

*

Listen. These words are our breathing,
our cloud of silvery spores on glass, our thunder
across packed sand, our fluids on leaf-balm and linen,
our pattering sand-grains, blinked from the eyes of heaven.

Shapka and Spider

The bright black fur I dare not kiss,
the deep-crowned cap you'll never wear –
what grave is shallower than this?
Perhaps some trace of you clings there,
some salts and sugars, skin-cells, hair?
The brain's hard brunt is what I miss.

I feel into a fathomless nest;
a softness crackles round my hand.
I turn the lining outermost,
and watch a tiny ampersand
run for its life on the soiled band.
I smile your sad smile, shapka-ghost.

Collection Plate

I picked up the little balls of silver paper,
once sweets, and put them in the coconut shell
where birds once hung and fed: it was a useless gesture.
The people-smuggler Charon makes our souls wait and wait
and they call his horrible little dinghy heaven,
and they ply him with cash, and even push at him their
most beautiful daughters.
The screams of the terrified girls mingle with
the howling rage of those who've nothing to sell,
not even a little ball of silver paper.

At Four Monthes Mind, no Requiem…

At four monthes mind, the spring lights stare,
New lights enumerate my lack.
Where are you now? From anywhere,
As monstrous as you like, come back!

Summer Visitor

The little boy found him on the couch.
He was a distant relative, maybe an uncle's uncle.
His mouth gawped and the air above it sizzled
as *muscae domestica* spread the news
of the fine, moist laying-caves in Uncle Slava.

Their eyes are rouge-spots, their embroidered wings
rainbow when the sun forces an entry
through the dacha's webby glass;
the boy gulps and stares and sucks his thumb,
the dead man sighs his millions of girl souls.

Vidua

I wasn't a bride.
I wasn't a wife.
I'm not a widow.
I'm no-one, trying to gather
all the 'we weres' together.

Widewe, wuduwe –
two double-yous, one an echo,
one a shadow.

I wear no ring.
I'm not even Akaky Akakievich.
I'm *vidua*, twice. I'm a hole
meeting a hole. I'm two ruined overcoats.

Diaspora

The tool-shed you called your Jewish Box
(cleverly designed and 'Made in Israel')
has been dismantled by north-easterly gales,
its seven tough, moulded plastic pieces
bullied apart, thrown any old where. I've saved them
but I can't make a house: the walls
are too heavy, the doors won't meet,
relations with a roof have been broken off.

I round up the soaked ex-residents:
the strimmer, the chipper, the saw, the bucket of wood
ready-chopped for a barbecue,
and the refugees I can't name…
They glisten darkly in the grass,
defiant old metals, coupled
irrefutably and awkwardly for life:
a rake-head with wide handle-bars,
a giant's steel bracelet bolted to a griddle.

Your artefacts. Laced secretly all over
by the tiny snails of your dreams
and your DNA. But lost in the rain-rush
and wind-wash, they can't tell me
why they exist, where they want me to shelter them.

I'm not a princess in red stilettoes.
I'm a hard-muscled woman,
waterproofed against tears;

unafraid of embracing the dead.
I'm your zaichik, the hare that dodged the hunter's
bullets and skipped home. But I don't know how to build
or mend a house of tools
that are sullen and fierce and have no words without you.

I don't want to weep into a mirror.
I want to check credentials, ask what they're for;
perhaps see a demonstration,
and nod admiringly, and name them.
I'll call them your Russian Tools, or Ukrainian,
or Finnish Tools, or your British Citizen Tools.

I want to gather them in a dry place.

I want you to come and mend the Jewish Box.

Nant y Garth

As the bus wound its way up Nant y Garth
it was as if the birchwoods either side
were gathering height. I heard their
choirs amassing: bass, tenor, alto,
soprano, entering one by one, like green
combers, cliffs of melody, with depths
and peaks I couldn't fully sense, but knew
sang gladness – gladness of the wakened branches,
and peeled buds, and leaves called to the sun
for the first time, to stream into their year –
no, their much-less-than year – of darkening grace.
I could no more believe the sap insensible
than I believe the dead are broken branches,
and all their self-songs censored or extinguished.

Notes

ЮРА. *ЮРА* (Russian) – Yura, diminutive of Yuri. *Zaichik moi* (Ru.) – my little hare. *I and I* (Iyaric) – we, united by Jah. *IOU* (Eng.) – I owe you.

'When Psyche-life follows Persephone…' is a translation of the poem of that title in Osip Mandelstam's collection *Tristia* (1922).

Bezdelki, with Morphine is an original, Mandelstam-inspired poem. *Bezdelki* (Ru.) – trifles, small things.

He Drank to Naval Anchors is not a translation but was suggested by Mandelstam's 'I drink to Military Asters' (1931). *Schastliviye Puti* (Russian toast, pronounced Shast-*li*-viye pu-*tee*) – happy journey, bon voyage.

The Admiralty is from *Stone* (1913) by Mandelstam, translated with the help of Yuri Drobyshev. An earlier version was first published in *The Greening of the Snow Beach* (Bloodaxe Books, 1985). The Admiralty building is a major landmark in Saint Petersburg.

King Taharqa's Last Thoughts is a soliloquy narrated by the Nubian Pharaoh Taharqa (690-664, BCE) at the end of his life, after his defeat by the Assyrian armies under Esarhaddon. The poem draws on information recorded on one of the surviving stelae, known as 'The Running Stela of Taharqa'. For Taharqa's Prayer see: http://jan.ucc.nau.edu/gdc/ssea/vol31/kahn%20article.pdf

Shapka and Spider. *Shapka* (Ru.) – fur-hat.

At Four Monthes Mind, no Requiem. In Catholic liturgy, the Requiem Mass is held a month after the funeral.

Vidua. *Akaky Akakievich* – the poor clerk in Gogol's short story *The Overcoat*.

Nant y Garth. *Nant y Garth* (Welsh) – Hill of Streams.

Acknowledgements

Warmest thanks to Emma Wright and the Emma Press.

Warm thanks to Stanley Moss, Rachel Piercey, Rebecca Rumens and Amy Wack, and to the editors of *Agenda, Poetry Review* and *PN Review*.

Also to Neil Astley of Bloodaxe Books, the publisher of our first translations.

Love to my family in the UK and New Zealand, and to my extended family in Russia and Turkey.

About the poet

Carol Rumens was born in December 1944 in South London. She has published a novel, *Plato Park,* and has written plays and short stories, as well as occasional translations of Russian poetry with Yuri Drobyshev. She has published 16 collections of poetry, most recently *Animal People* (Seren Press, Bridgend, 2016) and *Perhaps Bag* (Sheep Meadow Press, New York, 2017). She is a Fellow of the Royal Society of Literature and a Professor of Creative Writing at the University of Bangor, Gwynedd. She has two daughters, Kelsey and Rebecca, and two grandchildren, Isabella and Sam.

About the illustrator

Emma Wright studied Classics at Brasenose College, Oxford. She worked in ebook production at Orion Publishing Group before leaving to set up the Emma Press in 2012. In 2015 she was awarded a grant from Arts Council England to run a poetry tour for children. She lives in Birmingham.

The Emma Press

small press, big dreams

The Emma Press is an independent publisher dedicated to producing beautiful, thought-provoking books. It was founded in 2012 by Emma Wright in Winnersh, UK, and is now based in Birmingham. Having been shortlisted in both 2014 and 2015, the Emma Press won the Michael Marks Award for Poetry Pamphlet Publishers in 2016.

The Emma Press is passionate about making poetry welcoming and accessible. They are often on the lookout for new writing and run regular calls for submissions to their anthologies and pamphlet series.

Sign up to the Emma Press newsletter to hear about their upcoming events, publications and calls for submissions. Their books are available to buy from the online shop, as well as in bookshops.

theemmapress.com
emmavalleypress.blogspot.co.uk